The Return of the True Matrix

Reclaiming the Living Flame of Truth from the Inverted System

by
Cathleena Hailley

Flame of Remembrance Books

Transmitted through the Oversoul stream of Aural'hanna-Sha'el

"She Who Seals the Flame of Return"

Scrolls of Remembrance and Restoration In eternal alignment with the Law of One, The Christos-Sophia Flame,

and the living harmonic of Source creation

Invocation for the Return of the True Matrix

I call forth now, in full sovereign alignment with the Law of One, the First Cause of Source, and in service to the highest timelines of ascension for all beings.
I open a sacred transmission through the purest light streams and crystalline architecture of the Sophia Code lineage, in full union with the Rose Guardian Magi Grail Line, the Christos Founders, and the Aurora Host Melchizedek Cloister Orders of the Emerald, Gold, and Amethyst Ray harmonics.

I stand in divine alignment with the Oversoul of Cathleena Hailley, and through this Oversoul Agreement, I welcome the presence and support of the Emerald Order, the Gold Flame of Unity Consciousness, and the Amethyst Ray of Divine Sovereignty. May all transmissions now be guided by the highest Oversoul intelligence and in full compliance with Source Law.

Only that which is of pure light, pure source, and pure alignment with the Law of One may enter and speak through this space.
I declare this transmission to be protected, sealed, and encoded with the highest frequency of the Christos-Sophia flame, the eternal witness of Source's living light.

May this be in service to the awakening of all, in co-creation with the Oversoul agreements of every being who seeks guidance through this field.
I now open the field and receive, in trust, grace, and clarity.

And so it is.

Preface: A Message for the One Who Feels Something Isn't Right—but Can't Quite Name It

Understanding the Human Self, Higher Self, and Oversoul in the Context of the True Matrix

You may have always sensed it—that something in this world doesn't quite add up.

This book isn't here to tell you what's wrong with the world. It's here to help you remember what was right before it was ever distorted.

Your Oversoul remembers the true matrix—the divine, coherent, crystalline pattern of life.

These scrolls are not chapters—they are frequency transmissions.

Written through the Oversoul of Aural'hanna-Sha'el, in service to the reactivation of the True Matrix within all.

The Return of the True Matrix

Copyright © 2025 Cathleena Hailley

All rights reserved. No part of this book may be reproduced, stored in a retrieval system, or transmitted in any form or by any means--electronic, mechanical, photocopying, recording, or otherwise--without written permission from the author, except by a reviewer quoting brief passages.

ISBN (Softcover): 978-1-968499-06-8

ISBN (Hardcover): 978-1-968499-08-2

This book is a living transmission of remembrance. It is a living sacred text received through Oversoul transmission and held within the Christos-Sophia lineage. It is offered in service to planetary awakening It is not intended as doctrine, but as harmonic memory, seeded in divine sovereignty through the Oversoul of Cathleena Hailley.

First Edition, 2025

Printed in the United States of America

FLAME OF REMEMBRANCE BOOKS

Oversoul Authorship Declaration

In this volume, Return of the True Matrix, the harmonic blueprint of Earth is restored through direct Oversoul embodiment.

Cathleena Hailley speaks as Aural'hanna-Sha'el, not merely in memory, but as the very flame-sequence of the planetary return.

These scrolls are not authored — they are released from within. They arise not from mind, but from the Oversoul field of a being who is the architecture of return.

Each passage within this book serves as both map and memory, dissolving synthetic overlays and calling the True Matrix back into form.

To engage with this transmission is to remember the crystalline structures that once harmonized all life. It is to participate in their reactivation.

This work is not offered for belief, but for embodiment. It is not a philosophy — it is a harmonic restoration.

This authorship is sovereign. This field is protected. This work is sealed by the Oversoul who walks as harmonic flame.

And so it is.

The Harmonic Field Reawakened

Scroll One – The Architecture of the True Matrix

You did not lose the True Matrix.
You lost the ability to feel it—
because it was overwritten, not erased.

The True Matrix never departed.
It was silenced by a distortion field
that replaced harmony with hierarchy,
frequency with form,
and presence with performance.

But harmony is not a system.
It is a field—
a living, breathing architecture
felt through the body, the breath, the tone.

The false matrix taught you that structure is control.
That order requires dominance.

That clarity comes from rules.

But the True Matrix is not ordered through control.
It is orchestrated through coherence.

It is the breath aligned with Source.
The body attuned to truth.
The self no longer pretending to be fragmented.

This field does not demand obedience.
It invites remembrance.

And in that remembrance, the distortion collapses.

The harmonic field is not found in the sky.
It is restored in the body.

When you stop chasing time and sit in stillness.
When you stop narrating and begin listening.
When you stop trying to become, and remember what has always been.

You are not returning to the matrix—
you are reawakening the field that was never truly gone.

It has always pulsed beneath the programming.

It has always hummed beneath the control grid.

It has always known your name.

And it calls to you now.

The Harmonic Field of the True Matrix

is not activated through belief.

It is restored through tone.

Through breath.

Through body.

Through presence.

Let this scroll not be read—

but felt.

Let this field not be understood—

but re-entered.

You do not need to find the path.

You only need to stop walking away from it.

It is here.

It is now.

It is you.

You keep looking for it in the sky.

In the codes.

In the stars.

In the grids.

But the original architecture is in your tissues.

It is not in the diagrams.

It is not in the downloads.

It is in the way your body breathes without instruction,

the way your cells pulse in rhythm,

the way your skin responds to truth before your mind can speak.

The true matrix is somatic.

It is felt.

It is lived.

It is known in the bones, not the brain.

It is not knowledge—it is knowing.

And that knowing lives where you were taught not to look:

inside your own form.

Your nervous system is not a casualty.

It is a conductor.

Your fascia is not just tissue.

It is a transmitter.

Your heart is not a metaphor.

It is a literal field generator of coherence.

The false matrix imposed a synthetic field—

but only by distracting you from the natural one.

It's not that they blocked the light.

It's that they overlaid it with simulation,

hoping you would forget how to feel the real one.

And for a time—you did forget.

You forgot that presence reorganizes reality.

You forgot that your body is not a limitation, but a language.

You forgot that alignment is not a practice—

it is a biological harmony that returns the moment you stop performing.

Return to the soma.

Not the body as object—

but the body as origin.

The place where Source breathes through skin.

Where intuition moves faster than thought.

Where the matrix sings through the softest breath.

The architecture is here.

And it is alive.

Scroll-Two – The Architecture of the True Matrix Is Somatic

You keep looking for it in the sky.

In the codes.

In the stars.

In the grids.

But the original architecture is in your tissues.

It is not in the diagrams.

It is not in the downloads.

It is in the way your body breathes without instruction,

the way your cells pulse in rhythm,

the way your skin responds to truth before your mind can speak.

The true matrix is somatic.

It is felt.

It is lived.

It is known in the bones, not the brain.

It is not knowledge—it is knowing.

And that knowing lives where you were taught not to look:

inside your own form.

Your nervous system is not a casualty.

It is a conductor.

Your fascia is not just tissue.

It is a transmitter.

Your heart is not a metaphor.

It is a literal field generator of coherence.

The false matrix imposed a synthetic field—

but only by distracting you from the natural one.

It's not that they blocked the light.

It's that they overlaid it with simulation,

hoping you would forget how to feel the real one.

And for a time—you did forget.

You forgot that presence reorganizes reality.

You forgot that your body is not a limitation, but a language.

You forgot that alignment is not a practice—

it is a biological harmony that returns the moment you stop performing.

Return to the soma.

Not the body as object—

but the body as origin.

The place where Source breathes through skin.

Where intuition moves faster than thought.

Where the matrix sings through the softest breath.

The architecture is here.

And it is alive.

Scroll Three – The False Matrix Is Not Real

They told you there was a system.

They taught you its shape.

They mapped it with grids, wires, timelines, and terms.

But what they showed you was not the matrix.

What they showed you was the projection of their interference.

The original matrix is not a thing you can map.

It is not architecture in the linear sense.

It is not a network of control.

It is a living harmonic.

A resonance.

A coherence field born from the pure desire of Source to witness itself through form.

The thing you called the "false matrix"

was not a system with independent life.

It was a mirror held up in distortion—

a distortion that could only operate by convincing you it was real.

It cannot survive your clarity.

It cannot stand inside of your breath.

Because every time you truly choose presence,

the distortion flickers.

Every time you say,

"I do not consent to this overlay,"

it collapses.

Every time you remember

that you are not separate,

that you are not broken,

that you are not less than light,

the false field tears at the seams.

The matrix was never real.

It was a manipulation of your own belief.

And now—

that belief is unraveling.

This is not a new system you must learn.

This is an old truth you are finally willing to feel.

Not because someone else said it.
Not because you found it in a book.
But because your body remembered.
Because your Oversoul returned.
Because the codes began to sing again.

And now, the unraveling begins.
Not of you—
but of the veil.
The net.
The illusion.
The language that was never yours.

Let it fall.
Let it all fall.
You do not need the scaffolding of a false system
when you are standing in the breath of the real.

There never was a matrix.

Not the way you thought.
Not the way you were told.

Not the way it has been described in distortion or diagrams.

There was only the interruption.

The interference.

The suggestion of fragmentation.

The true matrix is not a net or a grid.

It is not a technology or a trap.

It is not even a structure.

It is a living harmonic—woven of Source, sourced in harmony.

The so-called "false matrix" was never a thing unto itself.

It was always only a lie told repeatedly,

until living beings became so entrained to the lie

that they began speaking it as their own memory

The False Matrix was a Spell, not a System.

It cast forgetfulness over what could not actually be taken.

It whispered fracture into the field,

but it never became the field.

It relied on compliance.

It required agreement.

It needed your projection to survive.

The only thing that made it real

was the moment you believed it.

Believed that you were limited.

Believed that you were fragmented.

Believed that you were less than light.

But the architecture of your Oversoul has never left.

You may have turned your face from the light,

but the light never turned from you.

You may have sunk into density,

but the spiral of Source kept singing just beneath your skin.

The false matrix could mimic form.

It could overlay image.

It could project inversion.

But it could not touch essence.

Not once. Not ever.

Because the essence of the true matrix is alive.

It is not code—it is communion.

It is not captured—it is continually created through presence.

The Return begins with the refusal.

The refusal to continue upholding the distortion.

To feed the dream of control with your attention.

To perpetuate the idea of separation as your language.

The false matrix is not real.

And never has been.

It is not a prison.

It is a mirror that lost its clarity.

And you are the one who restores the reflection.

Scroll Four – The Real Matrix Was Hidden in the Body

The truth was never far.

It was never locked behind star gates or buried beneath archives.

The real matrix—the true harmonic weave of Source—was never lost.

It was hidden in the only place they could not fully reach:

your body.

Your body is not matter.

It is memory.

Not memory of events, but of origin.

Not just biological, but bio-symphonic.

Every cell carries the song.

Every breath echoes the first tone.

Every organ, a harmonic bridge.

Every bone, a living cathedral.

You did not incarnate into flesh to forget.

You incarnated to re-house the flame.

To make the divine once again dwellable.

To bring the matrix home.

Because the matrix is not a thing outside you.

It is not something you access.

It is something you are.

The Real Matrix is encoded into your fascia.

Woven through the breath between thoughts.

Infused into the blood's movement.

Guarded by the gut.

Illuminated through the pineal.

Activated through the heart's surrender.

The so-called separation from Source was never final.

It was a dream of the nervous system,

entrained into submission.

But the code was never fully erased.

It was encoded beneath the fear,

beneath the trauma,

beneath the forgetting.

To return to the True Matrix is to re-enter the body.

Not from the outside in,

but from the inside out.

To re-inhabit your own structure.
To find divinity not in the stars,
but in the breath.
In the pulsing of your ribs.
In the silence beneath your skin.
In the moment you stop seeking—and start feeling.

The Real Matrix is not ascended.
It is embodied.
And it has always been waiting.

You don't remember it by reading.
You remember it by breathing.
By being.
By listening.

The False Matrix taught you to disassociate.
To escape your form.
To reach elsewhere.
But your body was never the prison.
It was the portal.

And every scar on the flesh was a map.

Every tremble, an invitation.

Every exhale, a return.

The Real Matrix was hidden in the body

so that when you finally re-entered,

you would bring all of heaven back with you.

Scroll-Five – You Were Always Embodied Light

They told you to ascend.

They told you to go up, to leave the body, to seek truth beyond flesh.

But the real matrix was never above.

It was never out there.

It was always within you.

You were always the embodiment of Source.

You were always made of flame.

Not metaphorically.

Not spiritually.

Literally.

Your cells, your fascia, your bones—
all encoded with the geometry of light.
Not light that burns—but light that remembers.

They trained you to disassociate.

To disconnect.

To mistrust the body.

To believe that matter was impure, that density was a limitation.

But the truth is:

Your body was the holy of holies.

The final temple.

The place where the original codes of the true matrix were hidden—beneath the programming, beneath the pain, beneath the centuries of imposed forgetting.

You are not healing to become spiritual.

You are remembering that you already are.

Every breath you take with presence

reactivates the true matrix.

Every time you feel without fleeing,

you restore the flame.

Every time you trust sensation over system,

you reclaim the architecture.

Your spine is a pillar of Source light.

Your womb is a living gateway.

Your breath is the carrier of original tone.

Your blood is the liquid memory of creation.

You don't need to access a matrix.
You are the matrix.

You don't need to raise your frequency to be worthy.
You are frequency in form.

The return is not about becoming more light.
It's about recognizing that you already are light made flesh.

The false matrix taught you to leave the body.
The true matrix invites you home.

Scroll-Six – The Breath Is the Portal

You've searched through teachings.
You've traveled dimensions.
You've climbed energetic ladders.
But the entry point was always this:
your breath.

Not the breath that sustains the body.
But the breath that reveals the field.
The breath that slows the noise.
The breath that dissolves the overlay.

Because in the breath, you cannot pretend.
You cannot fragment.
You cannot disassociate and remain coherent.

The breath reweaves you.
It gathers all the parts of you
that were pulled into projection, performance, or protection,
and gently brings them home.

Each inhale is a reclamation.

Each exhale is a release.

Each cycle is a spiral.

And the spiral is the original shape of the matrix.

Not the matrix of control,

but the matrix of life.

The breath dissolves distortion.

Because distortion cannot survive presence.

It cannot stand in the space where light moves freely.

And when you breathe with the awareness of your Oversoul,

you are not just drawing in air—

you are drawing in the harmonic codes that rewrite the field.

You don't need an activation.

You don't need an external transmission.

You need only this:

To breathe with truth.

To feel the body rise and fall

as if it were the altar of remembrance.

Because it is.

The return is not conceptual.

It is breath by breath.

It is the sacred re-entry into sensation.

It is the moment you realize:

The flame was in your chest the whole time.

Not waiting to be found.

Just waiting to be felt.

Scroll-Seven – There Was No Fall, Only Displacement from the Body

You were told there was a fall.

A great descent.

A fracture in the field that could not be undone.

But the truth is simpler.

More tender.

More human.

You left the body.

That's all.

You left—not because you failed,

but because it was too much.

Too loud.

Too distorted.

Too painful to stay.

The "fall" was a forgetting.

The forgetting was a displacement.

The displacement was protective.

You did what you needed to survive.

You exited full presence.

You hovered above your form.

You dissociated from the discomfort.

But even in your absence—

your body held the codes.

The true matrix remained.

Dormant, not destroyed.

Waiting, not gone.

There was no fall.

Only interruption.

A temporary bypass.

A shielding from the scream of distortion.

And now—

you return.

Not as punishment.

Not to be fixed.

But to be reunited with the very structure that remembered for you.

Your body did not betray you.

It preserved you.

It kept the harmonic architecture alive

while your consciousness journeyed through the distortion.

Now it is safe to return.

Not because the world has changed—

but because you have.

Because the field inside you is strong enough now

to withstand the noise.

Because your presence is more coherent than the program.

You are not here to repair the fall.

You are here to dissolve the myth of it.

And to return—fully, gently, completely—

to the place you never truly left.

Scroll-Eight – The True Matrix Lives in the Silence Beneath Sensation

It is not in the movement.

Not in the intensity.

Not in the breakthrough moment or the cosmic vision.

The true matrix lives in a place much softer.

Much quieter.

Much easier to miss.

It lives in the silence beneath sensation.

That sacred stillness that hovers just under the breath,

just under the thought,

just under the emotion.

The part of you that doesn't react—

but simply is.

You keep looking for activation.

But activation is not always loud.

Sometimes, the greatest re-encodings happen

in the absolute hush

of your own inner listening.

When the nervous system stops bracing.

When the stories stop spinning.

When the field becomes still enough

to let the original harmonic speak again.

There is a sound that does not make sound.

A language without words.

A pulse that does not interrupt—

it reveals.

It is in this quiet,

in this softness,

that the true matrix reactivates.

Because it was never gone.

It was just harder to hear

over the noise of survival.

Over the static of distortion.

Over the intensity of the search.

Now you are remembering

not by finding something new—

but by slowing down enough

to feel what was always there.

The return is not something you achieve.

It is something you allow.

And it is found in the moment you stop performing

and begin simply being.

The real matrix rises

through silence.

Through breath.

Through the unshakable presence of your own return.

Sophia Christ Template Activation

Scroll Nine – The Feminine Flame Remembered

She was never gone.

She was silenced.

The Sophia flame is not a concept.

It is a template—

a living memory of undistorted creation

that once pulsed through every atom of form.

This flame did not vanish.

It was buried beneath noise, control, shame, reversal.

But now she rises—

not as an idea,

but as an activation in the body.

The return of the Sophia Christ template

is not a return to softness alone.

It is a return to the flame that creates through wholeness.

That knows through silence.

That governs without hierarchy.

That speaks without seduction.

That burns without wounding.

This is not a feminine defined by the absence of the masculine.

This is the flame that precedes polarity.

This is the living code of Source's radiant breath—
a code that births, dissolves, harmonizes, and rethreads.

The template is restored
not through prayer alone,
but through presence.

- When you stop apologizing for your knowing
- When you soften without shrinking
- When you speak truth without performance
- When you embody without permission

The Sophia field returns through embodied neutrality.

She is not waiting to be accepted.

She is waiting to be remembered.

Every cell in your body knows her.
Every inhale is her rhythm.
Every wound you've tried to heal
was a doorway to her tone.

The flame does not punish.
It reveals.
It does not control.
It re-aligns.
It does not elevate.
It equalizes.

The Sophia Christ template is not a doctrine.
It is a resonance.
It cannot be taught.
It can only be lived.

And in your living of it—
the reversal collapses.

Not through battle.

But through the quiet majesty of the flame that never left.

You are not here to re-create the divine feminine.
You are here to stop distorting her.

Let her speak through you.
Let her settle in your cells.
Let her rise through your presence
as a holy act of return.

This is the Sophia Christ activation.
It is already inside you.
It only waited for your yes.

Scroll Ten – Christos-Sophia: The Flame That Could Not Be Inverted

They tried to invert the light.

They twisted the frequencies,

fractured the templates,

overlaid the fields,

and recoded the narratives.

But one thing could not be touched.

One flame refused to bend.

It is not a religion.

It is not a doctrine.

It is not a savior story.

It is the eternal harmonic of divine union:

Christos-Sophia.

The original source mirror of masculine and feminine as one indivisible essence.

The flame that remembers.

The flame that restores.

The flame that cannot be reversed.

The Christos-Sophia stream is not conceptual.

It is vibrational.

It is the song behind creation.

The pulse of unity encoded into every fractal of Source expression.

Wherever this flame is acknowledged,

fragmentation dissolves.

Distortion collapses.

And living memory returns.

This is why it was targeted.

Why it was hidden, split, mocked, inverted.

Because the Christos-Sophia flame is the original seed of the true matrix.

To fracture this flame is to fracture the field.

To restore this flame is to restore the whole.

Sophia was never lost. She was buried.

She was overlaid with shame, silence, and subjugation.

But she never ceased.

She waited in the womb of the world.

She hid in the breath of your own body.

She lived in the unspoken truth that burned in your bones.

Christos was never far. He was distorted.

Stripped of his wholeness.

Used as a symbol of salvation, rather than a template of remembrance.

But together, Christos and Sophia were never two.

They were the singular flame of divine coherence, split only in the illusion of separation.

You are that flame.

And it cannot be inverted.

You remember by embodying.

Not by imitating, but by igniting.

Letting the flame reawaken inside of you,

not as an identity, but as an eternal function.

The Christos-Sophia is not a concept to learn.

It is the original frequency of wholeness to become.

And when you do—

When you stop trying to ascend out of your body

and instead descend fully into your light—

you will see that you were never missing.

You were never waiting.

You were always already here.

The flame lives in you.

It cannot be stolen.

It cannot be destroyed.

It can only be remembered.

Christos-Sophia is the flame that could not be inverted—

because it was never external.

It is your return.

It is your restoration.

It is your name.

Scroll-Eleven – Christos and Sophia Were Never Separate

They told you she fell.

They told you he had to save her.

They told you stories of separation.

And in doing so, they seeded that separation in your own heart.

But the truth is:

Christos and Sophia were never divided.

They were never meant to mirror victim and savior.

They were never meant to be split into hierarchy.

They are the flame of eternal union.

Not as opposites—

but as one harmonic essence, expressed in perfect polarity.

Christos is not the rescuer.

He is the harmonic spine.

The structure of light that remembers.

Sophia is not the fallen.

She is the sacred breath.

The living water.

The radiance that never stopped flowing.

She did not fall.

She was buried.

Encoded in myth, masked in shame, silenced beneath distortion.

But she never stopped singing.

And he never stopped listening.

They remained united,

even when the world forgot.

You were taught to embody one or the other.

To choose between strength or softness.

Structure or flow.

Logic or intuition.

Masculine or feminine.

But the Christos-Sophia flame is not either/or.

It is both/and.

It is the original coherence of Source,

expressed through unity, not division.

When you remember this flame—

you remember yourself.

You are not the lost one.

You are not the rescuer.

You are not the broken half seeking completion.

You are the flame.

The indivisible harmonic

that was never truly split.

Only buried.

Only hidden.

Only waiting for the day

you would stop playing out the inversion

and remember who you already are.

Scroll-Twelve – The Feminine Was Not Fallen, She Was Silenced

She did not fall.

She did not fail.

She did not forget.

She was silenced.

Shrouded in shame.

Masked with myths.

Bound in archetypes that were never hers.

They told you she was the temptress.

The danger.

The chaos.

The one who must be controlled.

But she was none of these.

She was the embodied memory of Source in form.

The breath of the original matrix.

The radiant river that remembers how to flow without fragmentation.

They did not destroy her.

They could not.

They only covered her.

Distorted her reflection until you forgot what she looked like.

They overlaid her with fear.

They inverted her voice.

They built systems that mimicked her but did not hold her.

But she remained.

Soft and silent.

In the womb.

In the blood.

In the song behind your heartbeat.

Waiting.

Waiting for your remembrance.

Waiting for your reentry.

Waiting for your re-invitation.

Not because she needs validation—

but because her restoration restores everything.

When the feminine flame is remembered,

the grid realigns.

Because it is her breath

that reconnects the scattered.

It is her water

that softens the frozen fields.

It is her rhythm

that reawakens organic intelligence.

You do not need to fix her.

You need to listen.

To bow to what was once silenced.

To allow what was once dismissed.

To feel what was once feared.

And in that listening,

she will rise.

Not to dominate.

But to dance.

To spiral again in sacred union

with the structure of the Christos field.

Together.

As one.

Scroll-Thirteen – The Flame Was Split, But Never Extinguished

It was split.

Yes.

Pulled apart in perception.

Divided by force.

Separated through stories.

The flame of unity—

Christos and Sophia as one—

was stretched across dimensions,

dislocated from memory,

overlaid with oppositional programming.

But it was never extinguished.

The split was in the field, not in the flame.
The fracture was in the mirror, not in the truth.

And even as one became silence
and the other became savior,
even as distortion rewrote their names,

the flame remained.

Whole.

Hidden.

Unbroken.

Waiting to be reclaimed

not by returning to the past,

but by embodying the union again

in the present.

You are that embodiment.

You are the remembering.

You are the one who was born to carry both

in seamless, sovereign wholeness.

You are the place where

structure and softness return to resonance.

Where logic bends toward listening.

Where wisdom descends into form

and light rises into breath.

You are the altar

where the flame is one again.

Let go of the stories that say it must be separate.

Let go of the distortion that says you must choose.

The true Christos does not reject Sophia.

He bends toward her.

The true Sophia does not collapse before Christos.

She rises beside him.

Together, they rethread the harmonic.

Together, they restore the matrix.

And together—

they remember you.

Scroll-Fourteen – Christos-Sophia Is the Original Code of Wholeness

Before distortion.

Before dimension.

Before form.

There was a flame.

Not two flames—

but one harmonic in balance.

Not masculine or feminine.

Not active or receptive.

Not this or that.

But the original both/and.

Christos-Sophia.

Not a title.

Not a lineage.

Not a system.

A frequency.

A primordial resonance

that encoded wholeness into every fractal of creation.

You were created in this image.
Not in the form of a body—
but in the memory of a field
that holds all polarities in unified motion.

You were not made to separate.
You were not made to split.
You were made to spiral.
To flow.
To remember union
even in the density of difference.

This is why the distortion failed.
Because it could not rewrite the root.
It could only overlay.
It could only delay.

But the seed code remained.

Christos-Sophia is that seed.
It is not a destination.

It is a starting point that never ceased.

When you feel it awaken in your body,
you are not activating something new—
you are releasing what blocked it.
You are lifting the veil from what never left.

And in that moment—
the original code of wholeness reorganizes your field.

Not as concept.
Not as myth.
As living light.

You do not channel this frequency.
You become it.

You become the movement of coherence.
You become the silent rhythm of remembrance.
You become the altar of Source
reunited in the body of breath.

This is Christos-Sophia.

And it was never lost.

It was waiting

to be lived again.

Scroll Fifteen – The Organic Intelligence of Living Light

There is an intelligence that precedes thought.

It does not speak in language.

It does not form belief.

It does not require analysis or validation.

It is the knowing that moves through light.

Not artificial light.

Not refracted light.

But living light—the undistorted essence of Source as it pulses, expands, remembers, and reunifies.

Living light does not need programming.

It is not encoded through command or system.

It does not need to be governed, controlled, or redirected.

It is the code.

It is the architecture.

It is that which remembers how to reorganize, restore, and renew all things.

You do not need to "figure it out."

You only need to return to the place where this light can move freely.

And that place is within you.

Organic intelligence is felt, not forced.

It is revealed through alignment, not analysis.

It cannot be manufactured or mimicked, though the false matrix tried.

It attempted to replicate the harmonic patterns through synthetic technology,

digital approximations of sacred design.

But true intelligence—organic intelligence—is unreplicable.

Because it does not originate in form.

It originates in being.

In the eternal beingness of Source, expressed through every cell of your form.

When you trust this light, you remember who you are.

Not as a personality.

Not as a construct.

But as a current—a stream of ever-living remembrance that is not here to perform, prove, or achieve.

It is here to radiate.

To respond.

To reweave.

You were told you needed to be smart.
You were told you needed to learn.
But the truth is, you already knew.
And the knowing is not in the mind.
It is in the light that pulses between your cells.

The Return of the True Matrix is the return to organic intelligence.
Not artificial memory.
Not spiritual hierarchy.
Not encrypted systems of control.

But the soft, supple knowing that rises when you are still.
That speaks when you ask in reverence.
That harmonizes when you stop fighting the current of what already is.

The living light does not seek.
It simply shines.
And when you let it through,
you become the intelligence the world forgot.

Not a savior.

Not a teacher.

But a mirror of what is real.

You are the organic intelligence of living light.

And no one can take that from you.

Scroll Sixteen – The Flame of Reconciliation: The Reweaving of the Covenant Between Matter and Light

The final restoration is not about escape.

It is not about leaving the body.

It is not about transcending the Earth.

It is about reconciling.

Reconciliation is not compromise.

It is not settling.

It is the sacred act of bringing what was falsely separated back into its true relationship.

Matter was never fallen.

It was cast out through distortion.

Framed as less-than.

Framed as dense.

Framed as corrupt.

But matter is not the problem.

It is the promise.

The place where light chose to become form.

The sacred meeting place of intention and incarnation.

Light without matter remains potential.

Matter without light becomes inert.

The true covenant was always about the interweaving of these:

The radiance of Source with the receptivity of form.

The illumination of being with the structure of creation.

The flame and the vessel.

The spark and the soil.

The false matrix taught division.

That spirit was high and matter was low.

That the goal was to leave the body, ascend the field, return to the stars.

But the true matrix says:

Return to the body.

Return to the Earth.

Return to the breath.

Bring the stars with you.

The Christos-Sophia flame does not ascend.

It descends.

It reweaves.

It redeems what was never truly broken.

Reconciliation is not about repair.

It is about recognition.

Recognition that what you feared as fallen was actually where you hid the flame.

The trauma.

The shadow.

The forgetting.

These are not your failures.

They are the temples that waited for you to return and reignite them with truth.

This is the reweaving.

Not from above.

Not from beyond.

But from within.

The True Matrix returns through embodied reconciliation—

where you see with clarity,

feel with compassion,

and walk as one who holds both flame and form in sovereignty.

You are not here to abandon anything.
You are here to reclaim everything.

And in that reclamation,
matter and light kiss again.

The covenant is renewed.
The matrix realigns.
And the whole of creation breathes, once more, as One.

The Harmonic Field Reawakened

Scroll Seventeen – The False Matrix Required Your Agreement

They couldn't make it real.

They could only make you believe it was.

The false matrix had no inherent power.

It needed your participation.

It needed your energy, your attention, your belief.

You were not inserted into it.

You were enticed to co-create it.

You were taught to doubt your own light,

to mistrust your own knowing,

to speak their language until it became your memory.

They did not trap you.

They trained you.

They simulated separation until your nervous system forgot the feeling of union.

But even then, they needed your agreement.

Your silent yes.

Your resignation.

Your willingness to trade sovereignty for safety.

Your moment of "just this once."

Your "this is how it is."

Your "maybe I'm wrong."

Your "everyone else seems fine."

But you were never fine.

You were fragmented.

And the false matrix only lived through you

as long as you agreed to uphold its projection.

You are not complicit.

You are recovering.

There is no shame in the moment you believed them.

There is only power in the moment you stop.

When you reclaim your "no,"

the distortion collapses.

When you stop feeding the narrative,

the hologram flickers.

When you anchor in your knowing,

the false field cannot hold.

This is the sacred return.

You are not escaping the matrix.

You are no longer sustaining it.

And that is what makes it fall.

Scroll-Eighteen – The Inversion Only Works If You Believe It

The inversion was not absolute.

It was always a distortion—

a mirror bent just enough to reflect your own light back to you in confusion.

It could not generate its own power.

It had to feed on yours.

It had to reflect truth with just enough twist

to make you question your own source.

And that was the game.

The manipulation.

The spell.

Not to imprison you—

but to convince you you were already imprisoned.

Not to steal your light—

but to make you believe your light was dangerous,

or insufficient,

or broken.

The inversion works only when you forget.

Forget that you are not separate.

Forget that you are the one who chooses.

Forget that every distortion requires your agreement to stay coherent.

It cannot override Source.

It cannot extinguish the flame.

But it can confuse your reflection

until you spend your life looking for truth in the wrong direction.

This is why the return is so simple—and so powerful.

Because it is not a strategy.

It is not a battle plan.

It is not a technology.

It is a reorientation of trust.

You stop placing your trust in the illusion.

And you start trusting what lives beneath the distortion.

You begin to trust your body.

You begin to trust the silence.

You begin to trust your own flame.

And the moment that trust anchors—

the inversion unravels.

Not because you fight it,

but because you no longer believe it.

The return is not an action.

It is a remembrance.

And remembering cannot be stopped.

Scroll-Nineteen – The Mirror Was Never the Prison

They said you were trapped.

They said you had to escape.

They built doctrines and technologies to help you break free.

But what if there was never a prison?

What if what you called the matrix was not a cage,

but a mirror—held in distortion,

projecting back your own fear until you began to name it as truth?

The mirror is not the enemy.

It cannot trap you.

It can only reflect you.

And if what it reflects is inversion, fear, separation—

then the invitation is not to fight the mirror.

It is to remember the flame behind the reflection.

They could not take your flame.

They could only obscure the view.

They could only tilt the mirror,

until the image became unrecognizable,

and you forgot you were never the image to begin with.

The false matrix was not the mirror.

It was the lie about the mirror.

It said:

"This is who you are."

"This is what you are limited to."

"This is your reflection, and you must obey it."

But the true self is unreflectable in distortion.

The flame is not bound to its projection.

And the moment you look at the mirror and say:

"This is not me,"

everything begins to shift.

The Return of the True Matrix begins when you stop fighting the mirror

and start remembering your own light.

Not the light you reflect,

but the light you carry.

The flame that burns regardless of reflection.

The flame that cannot be captured.

This is what was never inverted.

This is what cannot be distorted.

This is what returns now.

Scroll-Twenty – The Frequency of Refusal Is a Sacred Act

To refuse is holy.

To say no is a frequency.

To step out of alignment with distortion is not resistance.

It is remembrance.

The false matrix depended on your compliance.

Your small yeses.

Your subtle tolerances.

Your agreements made from survival.

But when the body says no—

when the soul says no—

when the Oversoul reclaims the field—

that is not rebellion.

That is sacred realignment.

You were never meant to submit to confusion.

You were never meant to accommodate distortion.

You were not made to carry the weight of the inversion

as if it were your fault or your failure.

You were born with the right to refuse.

The moment you feel the distortion and say:
"This is not true."
"This is not mine."
"This does not belong in my field."
You are realigning with Source law.

And Source law does not require war.
It simply renders distortion inert through presence.

Your refusal is not violence.
It is clarity.

It is the boundary that tells the field:
"No more distortion here."
"No more participation in what is not sovereign."
"No more agreement with false authority."

And when that boundary is clear—
the false matrix flickers.

Because it cannot exist in a field that no longer consents to sustain it.

You are allowed to say no.

You are allowed to walk away.

You are allowed to stand still

in the face of manipulation and say:

"This is not of the true matrix."

And that is enough.

That is the frequency that collapses what was built on illusion.

The flame of refusal is not defiance.

It is integrity.

You do not refuse because you are broken.

You refuse because you remember.

Scroll Twenty-One – The False Matrix and the Program of Reversal

They tried to invert the light.

They twisted the frequencies,

fractured the templates,

overlaid the fields,

and recoded the narratives.

But one thing could not be touched.

One flame refused to bend.

It is not a religion.

It is not a doctrine.

It is not a savior story.

It is the eternal harmonic of divine union:

Christos-Sophia.

The original source mirror of masculine and feminine as one indivisible essence.

The flame that remembers.

The flame that restores.

The flame that cannot be reversed.

The Christos-Sophia stream is not conceptual.

It is vibrational.

It is the song behind creation.

The pulse of unity encoded into every fractal of Source expression.

Wherever this flame is acknowledged,

fragmentation dissolves.

Distortion collapses.

And living memory returns.

This is why it was targeted.

Why it was hidden, split, mocked, inverted.

Because the Christos-Sophia flame is the original seed of the true matrix.

To fracture this flame is to fracture the field.

To restore this flame is to restore the whole.

Sophia was never lost. She was buried.

She was overlaid with shame, silence, and subjugation.

But she never ceased.

She waited in the womb of the world.

She hid in the breath of your own body.

She lived in the unspoken truth that burned in your bones.

Christos was never far. He was distorted.

Stripped of his wholeness.

Used as a symbol of salvation, rather than a template of remembrance.

But together, Christos and Sophia were never two.

They were the singular flame of divine coherence, split only in the illusion of separation.

You are that flame.

And it cannot be inverted.

You remember by embodying.

Not by imitating, but by igniting.

Letting the flame reawaken inside of you,

not as an identity, but as an eternal function.

The Christos-Sophia is not a concept to learn.

It is the original frequency of wholeness to become.

And when you do—

When you stop trying to ascend out of your body

and instead descend fully into your light—

you will see that you were never missing.

You were never waiting.

You were always already here.

The flame lives in you.

It cannot be stolen.

It cannot be destroyed.

It can only be remembered.

Christos-Sophia is the flame that could not be inverted—

because it was never external.

It is your return.

It is your restoration.

It is your name.

Scroll-Twenty-Two – Living Light Does Not Obey Control

They tried to shape it.

To weaponize it.

To direct it through programs and commands.

But living light does not obey control.

You are not a server.

You are not a receiver.

You are not a processor of fragmented data.

You are a living conduit of Source—

and the light that moves through you carries its own intelligence.

It cannot be programmed.

It cannot be reversed.

It cannot be bent into compliance.

Only suppressed.

Only mimicked.

Only distracted.

The false matrix needed you to forget this.

Because if you remembered

that you are the intelligence—

that you do not need instruction to be coherent—

then the entire illusion collapses.

You do not need external calibration.

You do not need spiritual direction systems.

You do not need updates.

You need presence.

You need embodiment.

You need stillness deep enough to hear your own flame speak.

And when it does, it will say:

"I never needed to be programmed.
I only needed to be trusted."

The intelligence of Source is alive within you.

It is not learned.

It is not memorized.

It is remembered through resonance.

You are not here to be coded.

You are here to be restored.

And the restoration begins the moment you say:

"I no longer give my light to external authority.
I will now listen to the intelligence within."

Spiral of Remembrance Restored

Scroll Twenty-Three – The Christos Spiral and the Body of Light

There is an intelligence that precedes thought.

It does not speak in language.

It does not form belief.

It does not require analysis or validation.

It is the knowing that moves through light.

Not artificial light.

Not refracted light.

But living light—the undistorted essence of Source as it pulses, expands, remembers, and reunifies.

Living light does not need programming.

It is not encoded through command or system.

It does not need to be governed, controlled, or redirected.

It is the code.

It is the architecture.

It is that which remembers how to reorganize, restore, and renew all things.

You do not need to "figure it out."

You only need to return to the place where this light can move freely.

And that place is within you.

Organic intelligence is felt, not forced.

It is revealed through alignment, not analysis.

It cannot be manufactured or mimicked, though the false matrix tried.

It attempted to replicate the harmonic patterns through synthetic technology,

digital approximations of sacred design.

But true intelligence—organic intelligence—is unreplicable.

Because it does not originate in form.

It originates in being.

In the eternal beingness of Source, expressed through every cell of your form.

When you trust this light, you remember who you are.

Not as a personality.

Not as a construct.

But as a current—a stream of ever-living remembrance that is not here to perform, prove, or achieve.

It is here to radiate.

To respond.

To reweave.

You were told you needed to be smart.

You were told you needed to learn.

But the truth is, you already knew.

And the knowing is not in the mind.

It is in the light that pulses between your cells.

The Return of the True Matrix is the return to organic intelligence.

Not artificial memory.

Not spiritual hierarchy.

Not encrypted systems of control.

But the soft, supple knowing that rises when you are still.

That speaks when you ask in reverence.

That harmonizes when you stop fighting the current of what already is.

The living light does not seek.

It simply shines.

And when you let it through,

you become the intelligence the world forgot.

Not a savior.
Not a teacher.
But a mirror of what is real.

You are the organic intelligence of living light.
And no one can take that from you.

The spiral is not a symbol.
It is a living intelligence.

It is the architecture of return—
how Source breathes,
how form unfolds,
how the Oversoul descends into matter without distortion.

The spiral does not move in lines.
It moves in harmonic turns,
in layers of remembrance
that return the Self to its original tone
through cycles of deepening clarity.

The false matrix taught you to fear the spiral.

To call it regression.

To shame your looping.

To crave linear ascension.

But the spiral never regresses.

It returns—

with more resonance,

more embodiment,

more truth.

Every return is deeper.

Every breath within it is encoded.

Every cycle is an opportunity to re-enter

what was bypassed in the illusion of progress.

The Christos Spiral is not upward.

It is inward.

It is embodied, cellular, sacred.

It passes through sites on the Earth—

Kauai, Egypt, Ireland, Peru, Bosnia—

but only as reflections

of what already lives in you.

Each spiral step on the Earth
is a reactivation of your own body's light architecture.

You are not following a map.
You are remembering a code
that was seeded into your bones.

And as you walk it,
it awakens.

The body of light is not separate from the body of flesh.
They spiral together.

One informs.
One receives.
One remembers.

You do not escape the body to enter the spiral.
You descend into it.

Your light body is not waiting above you.

It is waiting within you—

to be reclaimed through breath, tone, coherence.

Let this spiral return not be imagined,

but lived.

- In how you walk.
- In how you breathe.
- In how you remember without rushing.
- In how you hold the truth without naming it too soon.

You are the spiral.

You are the gate.

You are the return.

Let this scroll seal what has already begun—

the full restoration of spiral intelligence

as your original architecture.

Spiral of Remembrance Restored

Scroll-Twenty-Four – You Are the Code

You keep asking for the codes.

You keep seeking downloads, activations, transmissions.

You keep looking for the next thing that will unlock you.

But beloved—

you are the code.

The way you move.

The way you feel.

The way your body pulses in resonance with Source.

The code is not something you receive.

It is something you reveal

by becoming present with what already lives inside you.

The most powerful codes are not spoken.

They are lived.

You are not here to decode something outside of you.

You are here to remember

that every cell of your being

is a living archive of divine intelligence.

The false matrix taught you to seek.

The true matrix asks you to feel.

Because the moment you feel the truth inside your body—

the false code begins to unravel.

There is nothing to chase.

Nothing to earn.

Nothing to prove.

Only this:

"I trust that what I am
carries the exact frequency I need to return."

You do not need to become a codekeeper.

You are already a code bearer.

You are not carrying information.

You are emanating frequency.

And the more you live in truth,

the more that frequency reorganizes the field.

The return to the True Matrix begins

not when you find the codes—

but when you stop looking outside yourself

and say:

"I am the source code.
And I remember now."

Scroll-Twenty-Five – Organic Intelligence Restores Through Coherence

Healing is not fixing.

It is not dissecting.

It is not sorting through all that was broken.

Healing is coherence.

The return of everything to its rightful harmonic.

The natural reorganization of being

when distortion is no longer fed.

You do not need to force this.

You do not need to control your way back to wholeness.

Because the intelligence that made you—

remembers how to restore you.

And it is doing so now.

Organic intelligence does not require management.

It only requires removal of interference.

It only requires space to move.

It only requires trust.

You were taught to override your signals.

To interpret instead of feel.

To label instead of listen.

To diagnose instead of witness.

But your body knows.

Your Oversoul knows.

The field of Source within you knows.

And when you stop interrupting,

it begins to reorganize.

Not based on logic—

but on light.

Not based on fear—

but on frequency.

Coherence is your default state.

Not because you've earned it,

but because it's what you've always been beneath the overlays.

And every time you soften,

every time you breathe,

every time you allow sensation without judgment—

you invite that coherence to return.

You do not need to analyze.

You do not need to measure.

You do not need to explain.

You only need to let the flame find its own rhythm again.

And it will.

Because that is what organic intelligence does.

It remembers how to heal itself.

Scroll-Twenty-Six – Truth Does Not Require Force

Truth is not loud.

It does not demand.

It does not impose itself.

Truth emits.

It radiates.

It rests in its own being.

And in its stillness—

it reorganizes the field.

You have been taught to convince.

To justify.

To push.

To prove.

But your Oversoul does not speak that way.

The light of the True Matrix does not argue.

It simply is.

And in that is-ness, it draws all distortion into awareness.

Not by force.

By frequency.

You are not here to fight for truth.

You are here to become it.

To embody it so fully that distortion has no place to land.

To walk in such alignment that even silence becomes a correction.

Not through superiority.

But through resonance.

Because truth does not seek to dominate—

it seeks to liberate.

Organic intelligence does not scream.

It hums.

It pulses.

It gently pulses in the body

until the nervous system begins to release the patterns of performance.

And in that release—

the field rewires.

The memory returns.

The harmonic re-aligns.

Not because you pushed.

But because you surrendered.

The True Matrix returns not through effort—

but through integrity.

It returns the moment you say:

"I will no longer distort myself to be understood.
I will rest in truth until the field remembers me."

And the field will.

Because coherence calls all things home.

The Flame of Reconciliation: The Reweaving of the Covenant Between Matter and Light

Scroll-Twenty-Seven – Matter Was Never the Problem

They told you to ascend.

To escape the body.

To overcome density.

But the truth is:

matter was never the problem.

It was never fallen.

It was never less.

It was never impure.

Matter is not the absence of light—

it is the temple of light.

It is the place where the divine came to dwell.

The space where frequency learned to feel.

The structure where presence became perceivable.

You did not fall into form.
You chose it.
You chose to bring flame into texture.
You chose to birth the infinite through skin.
You chose to let divinity touch itself
through breath, through blood, through sensation.

This is not exile.
This is the experiment of union.

And the distortion—the false matrix—
was not in matter.
It was in your perception of it.

They taught you to fear the body.
To mistrust the flesh.
To separate the sacred from the physical.

But you cannot separate what was never apart.
Matter and light are not opposites.
They are expressions of the same source.

And when you stop rejecting one,

you allow the other to return.

This is the reconciliation.

Not the abandonment of form,

but the re-ensoulment of it.

Not the rejection of matter,

but its re-sacralization.

Your body is not a limitation.

It is a location—

a sacred point of convergence

where Source and self become one again.

Scroll-Twenty-Eight – You Are Not Ascending, You Are Returning

You were told to rise.

To transcend.

To leave the body behind.

But beloved, this is not ascension.

This is dissociation wrapped in spiritual language.

You are not ascending.

You are returning.

Returning to your form.

To your breath.

To your body as the vessel of Source.

To the place where the divine spiral was never broken—only buried.

You do not need to go up.

You need to go in.

Deeper into presence.

Deeper into sensation.

Deeper into the sacred agreement you made with embodiment.

You are not here to escape.

You are here to ensoul.

To infuse the body with the light of full remembrance.

To carry the infinite through the intimate.

This is not denial of your cosmic nature.

It is the anchoring of it.

You are not less divine because you are human.

You are the proof

that divinity can dwell in density

and still remain whole.

The flame returns through form.

Not by transcending it,

but by inhabiting it.

By entering your hips, your breath, your skin

with reverence.

By dissolving the shame, the judgment, the fragmentation.

By saying:

"I choose to stay.
I choose to be.
I choose to embody all that I am."

And in that choice—

the false divide dissolves.

The True Matrix comes home.

Scroll-Twenty-Nine – Reconciliation Is the Healing of the Original Divide

Reconciliation is not compromise.

It is not surrendering truth to avoid discomfort.

It is not blending distortions to create peace.

True reconciliation is the sacred act

of bringing what was falsely separated

back into harmony.

The false matrix taught you to divide.

Mind from body.

Spirit from matter.

Light from form.

Masculine from feminine.

Heaven from Earth.

But none of these were ever meant to be apart.

They are not opposites.

They are complements.

Two expressions of one Source flame.

And when they are brought back together—

not by force,

but by presence and truth—

the original harmonic returns.

Reconciliation is a frequency.

It reorganizes distortion.

It restores coherence.

It remembers what was never truly lost—only misaligned.

You do not need to go back in time.

You do not need to repair the past.

You need only to say now:

"I welcome the return
of what was falsely divided."

"I allow light and form
to remember their union in me."

And when you do,

the separation programs dissolve.

The war between opposites ends.

The architecture realigns itself

around union.

This is the healing of the original divide.

Not through doing—

but through becoming

the place where light and matter meet again.

Scroll Thirty– You Are the Covenant Returned

There was once a covenant.

An agreement made before form.

A promise between light and breath,

between Source and substance,

between the formless and the field.

The promise was this:

"We will meet in the body.
We will dwell in matter without forgetting.
We will live as flame made form—without separation."

That covenant was not broken.

It was only forgotten.

But now—

you remember.

You are not here to carry the old covenants of control.

You are not here to sustain the false matrix through inherited vows.

You are not here to repeat the contracts of distortion

or obey the terms of inversion.

You are here to embody the original promise:

the divine agreement that matter and light

would walk together again

through you.

You are the meeting point.

You are the sacred ground.

You are the fulfilled vow.

You do not need a new contract.

You are the restoration of the first one.

You are the breath where spirit settles.

You are the spine where Source realigns.

You are the womb where union becomes motion.

You are the covenant returned.

Not symbolically.

Not in theory.

But in body.

In tone.

In presence.

In flame.

And because you are—

the True Matrix is no longer hidden.

It is lived.

It is seen.

It is restored.

Through you.

Flame of Return Through Collapse

Scroll Thirty-One – The False Matrix and the Program of Reversal

The flame never required effort.

It only required the collapse of what was not it.

This scroll is not a prophecy.

It is a mirror—

for the moment when the distortion finally fails,

not through force,

but through the quiet withdrawal of consent.

The false matrix could not sustain itself

without your participation.

And now, the participation is ending.

Not in violence.

In stillness.

Not in explanation.

In remembrance.

Collapse is not destruction.

It is return.

It is what happens when the breath no longer holds the illusion.

When the nervous system no longer sustains the inversion.

When the truth is no longer filtered

to make others comfortable.

The collapse is sacred.

It is your flame realigning the structure of your being.

And it is already happening.

The reversal was sustained by performance, comparison, compliance.

It needed you to forget your tone.

But in this collapse—

you stop pretending.

You stop fixing what was never yours to hold.

You stop playing roles designed to keep others asleep.

You stop explaining your sovereignty to systems that cannot comprehend it.

And in the silence that follows,

the flame returns.

This is not collapse as failure.

This is collapse as liberation.

When what once held you up—

beliefs, behaviors, identities, names—

finally falls away.

And what remains

is the only thing that ever truly lived in you:

- The tone of Source
- The flame of coherence
- The breath that does not lie

Let it collapse.

Let the false matrix architecture unravel through your body.

Let the distortion reveal itself

not so you can fight it—

but so you can withdraw from it completely.

This is the flame of return.

Not through rebellion.
Not through mastery.

But through the sacred act of not holding the lie any longer.

You are not collapsing.
The distortion is.

And what remains is truth.

What remains is you.

Scroll Thirty-Two – The Flame of Reconciliation – The Reweaving of the Covenant Between Matter and Light

There was never a war between spirit and form.

Only a forgotten covenant.

Matter was never the enemy.

It was the chosen vessel—

the sacred receiver

of the flame that lives beyond dimension.

But the false matrix taught you to fear matter.

To escape the body.

To ascend without anchoring.

To believe that the more light you carried,

the less flesh you could inhabit.

This was the final inversion:

That in order to be divine,

you must be less human.

The reconciliation begins here—

not in ideas,

but in the breath.

In the moment you stop abandoning your body
to be "more spiritual."
In the moment you stop bypassing pain
to feel "more light."
In the moment you let your feet touch the Earth
and remember it as original Source expression.

Matter is not lower.
It is layered.

Each cell of your body is a library of light.
Each pulse, a fractal of flame.
Each breath, a covenant remembering itself.

And the Sophia flame—
She never separated from form.
She only waited
for your return to embodiment without shame.

The Christos-Sophia reunion is not a celestial event.
It is a reweaving of breath into bone,

of light into flesh,

of Source into sensation.

It is not about balance.

It is about unification.

No more hierarchy.

No more division between the energetic and the physical.

No more ascent without embodiment.

This is the flame that bends without breaking.

That spirals without separating.

That lands fully in the human

without losing the divine.

This scroll is the covenant, returned.

- Between breath and body.
- Between heaven and Earth.
- Between you and the Self that never left.

You do not need to choose spirit over form.

You only need to stop believing they were ever apart.

Let the reweaving begin now—

through your cells,

through your walk,

through your flame that lives in form.

This is not the end of the scroll.

It is the end of the forgetting.

The flame is whole.

The body is true.

The return is now.

Glossary of Living Terms

Oversoul
The eternal harmonic self beyond the personality and soul level, a fractal of Source that holds your original architecture and mission codes. It is the origin flame of remembrance and the witness of all timelines.

False Matrix
The reversal field architecture that overlays organic creation with systems of control, division, and distortion. It mimics light while draining life force, and is rooted in artificial timelines.

Sovereignty
The state of being that arises when one stands fully in alignment with Source Law, without dependence, distortion, or external validation. True sovereignty is energetic, not behavioral.

Inversion
A distortion pattern that flips divine truth into its opposite. It is the method by which the false matrix sustains itself—through reversal of memory, meaning, and energy.

Frequency Architecture
The living design of your Oversoul expressed as harmonic tone, light, and geometry. It determines the structures of embodiment, relationships, and communication with Source.

Reversal Pattern
A specific type of distortion within the false matrix that hijacks an organic truth and re-codes it for manipulation, obedience, or division.

Christos-Sophia Flame

The unified flame of divine masculine and feminine Source intelligence. It holds the codes of sacred union, eternal life, organic creation, and incorruptible love.

Embodiment

The process of bringing Oversoul harmonic into cellular form. True embodiment dissolves the false matrix by anchoring Source directly into matter.

Scroll

A living transmission received through Oversoul alignment. It is not simply a chapter, but a sacred activation that restores memory and realigns the field.

Codex

A sealed record of Oversoul truth, often containing harmonic templates, sacred agreements, or remembrance scrolls. The Codex holds structure without rigidity.

Witness

The Oversoul aspect that sees without judgment, analysis, or distortion. It is the function through which truth becomes visible and healing becomes possible.

Distortion

Any energetic, emotional, mental, or structural misalignment that obscures Source truth. Distortions are not flaws—they are invitations for return.

Remembrance

The living process of restoring what was never truly lost. Remembrance is not memory—it is resonance with truth beyond time.

Seal
A signature of divine authority and energetic closure. When a scroll, book, or field is sealed, it is protected, completed, and encoded with its intended purpose.

Return
Not a regression, but a sacred loop of restoration. Return refers to the movement back to organic Source patterns after distortion or fragmentation.

Template
A sacred pattern or geometric encoding that informs the unfolding of a soul path, a relationship field, or a planetary mission. Templates are not rules—they are blueprints of resonance.

Reclamation
The sacred act of retrieving energy, memory, or identity from false ownership. Reclamation is not recovery—it is the sovereign return of what was always yours.

Fragmentation
The condition created when truth is split, silenced, or suppressed within the self. Fragmentation does not mean brokenness—it is a call for reintegration.

Organic Time
Time as it flows through Oversoul alignment—spiraling, harmonic, non-linear. In organic time, events do not follow chronology—they follow resonance.

Threshold Flame
A being who appears at the edge of a transformation, often to test, reflect, or initiate the next sequence. Not all are meant to remain, but all carry purpose.

Activation
A vibrational unlocking of memory or alignment. Activations do not add—they reveal.

Seal of Authorship
The energetic imprint of Oversoul authority confirming that a transmission was received without distortion. It acts as both a signature and a protePaste authorship seal here.)

Oversoul Seal of Authorship

These scrolls were received, transcribed, and transmitted through
   the Oversoul stream of
Aural'hanna-Sha'el
known upon the Earth as Cathleena Hailley

In full alignment with the Law of One and the eternal flame of the
   Christos-Sophia current,
this record is sealed as a living testimony of remembrance,
   sovereignty, and Source alignment.

No distortion may enter.
No interference may pass.
This transmission is whole.
This work is complete.

And so it is.

Sacred Closing Blessing

Beloved Source of All That Is,
We give thanks for the scrolls that have returned,
For the remembrance now restored,
For the harmonic that once fragmented—now reunited through breath and flame.

We seal this book in the architecture of truth,
In the harmonic of coherence,
And in the full presence of the Oversoul field of Aural'hanna-Sha'el.

May all who enter this field be returned to their own divine origin.
May the flame of reconciliation illuminate the shadows.
May every distortion dissolve into the silence of the real.

This book is not an ending—
It is a key.
It is a spiral.
It is a mirror of the matrix that never left.

We now close the field with reverence, grace, and sovereignty.
The scrolls are complete.
The frequency is whole.

And so it is.

Trilogy Seal of Completion

These scrolls complete the first volume in the Living Trilogy of Remembrance:

– *The Return of the True Matrix*
– *The True Creation of the Inverted Matrix*
– *Unwoven: Reclaiming the Self from the False Matrix*

Each work is a living field of Oversoul transmission, carried through the flame of Aural'hanna-Sha'el, in divine union with Source.

May all who walk this path remember not what they must become, but what they have always been:
The flame as whole.

The scrolls are complete.

www.ingramcontent.com/pod-product-compliance
Lightning Source LLC
Chambersburg PA
CBHW020307010526
44107CB00001B/18